Letters to My Younger Self

Shaheen Dil

Gyroscope Press

This publication is a creative work protected in full by all applicable copyright laws. No part of this book may be reproduced or transmitted in any form or by any means, electronic or mechanical, including photocopying, recording, or by any information storage and retrieval system without the written permission of Gyroscope Press, except in the case of brief quotations embodied in critical articles or reviews or where permitted by law. All rights reserved.

Gyroscope Press
PO Box 1989
Gillette, WY 82717
gyroscopepress@gmail.com

Letters To My Younger Self
Copyright © 2025 by Shaheen Dil
Cover Image by David Muenzer © 2025
Author photo by JMKL Creative © 2025
Cover Design, Interior Layout by Constance Brewer

ISBN: 978-1-7367820-6-4
Published in the United States of America

For my children

David Sikander Muenzer
and
Maya Miriam Muenzer

The light of my eyes

Acknowledgements

My sincere thanks to Constance Brewer and Gyroscope Press for their faith in this manuscript. Thanks also to my fellow workshop members who have provided feedback on many of these poems over the past few years: Michael Wurster and the other members of the Pittsburgh Poetry Exchange, the US1 Poetry Exchange, and of course, the Porch Poets. I am grateful for their ongoing support and community.

Thanks also to my husband, Clark Muenzer, who introduced me to Paul Celan and reads and critiques everything I write, to my poet-friends Lyubomir Nikolov and Leyla Colpan, who reviewed this manuscript in a late draft, and my son, David Muenzer, who made the intriguing cover for this book. Last but definitely not least, a special thanks to my friend and fellow poet, Ziggy Edwards, who patiently read and commented on multiple versions of this manuscript.

I also want to acknowledge the journals and editors who have published some of these poems, sometimes in slightly different forms:

Parts of Letter 2 first appeared in *Constellations*, Fall/Winter Issue, 2024.

Letters 3, 10, and 20 (under other titles) appeared in different issues of *Uppagus*, 2024.

A slightly different version of Letter 14 under the title "Twinkies" appeared in *Gyroscope Review*, Fall Issue 2024.

Slightly different forms of Letters 16 and 39 first appeared in *Acts of Deference*, 2016, as "Nanni's Advice" and "Ephemera."

Table of Contents

Pittsburgh, Pennsylvania, 2024

    Letter 1 _____ 5

Old Dhaka, East Pakistan, 1954

    Letter 2 _____ 6

    Letter 3 _____ 7

    Letter 4 _____ 8

    Letter 5 _____ 10

    Letter 6 _____ 12

    Letter 7 _____ 13

    Letter 8 _____ 14

    Letter 9 _____ 16

    Letter 10 _____ 17

Karachi, West Pakistan, 1959

    Letter 11 _____ 18

Chicago, Illinois, 1959

    Letter 12 _____ 19

    Letter 13 _____ 21

Ann Arbor, Michigan, 1960

    Letter 14 _____ 23

    Letter 15 _____ 25

    Letter 16 _____ 26

    Letter 17 _____ 27

Lahore, West Pakistan, 1962

Letter 18 28

Letter 19 29

Letter 20 30

Swat Valley, Northwest Frontier Province, 1963

Letter 21 32

Abbottabad, West Pakistan, 1964

Letter 22 34

Bloomington, Indiana, 1966

Letter 23 35

Columbia, Missouri, 1967

Letter 24 36

Poughkeepsie, New York, 1968

Letter 25 39

Letter 26 40

Letter 27 41

Letter 28 43

Boston, Massachusetts, 1969

Letter 29 44

New York, New York, 1969

Letter 30 45

Poughkeepsie, New York, 1969

Letter 31 46

Letter 32 47

Washington, D.C, 1971
- **Letter 33** — 48
- **Letter 34** — 49
- **Letter 35** — 50
- **Letter 36** — 51
- **Letter 37** — 52
- **Letter 38** — 53

Princeton, New Jersey, 1973
- **Letter 39** — 54
- **Letter 40** — 55
- **Letter 41** — 56
- **Letter 42** — 58
- **Letter 43** — 59

Notes and Asides — 61

About the Author — 66

Abtrünning erst bin ich treu.
Ich bin du, wenn ich ich bin.
Paul Celan

Only if false am I true.
I am you, when I I am.
Tr. by Clark Muenzer

Choiti with the doll Ammu brought back from New Zealand.

Pittsburgh, Pennsylvania, 2024
Letter 1

Dear Choiti,

Where do you end and I begin?

I know the bend in the road you can't yet see,
      what lies past
           the hill rising.

You are prancing in tall grass;
      I am waking in a world you can't yet reach.

What was yours I now call mine,
      suspecting things may be the other way around.

Where might I end and you begin again?

Love,

Shaheen

Old Dhaka, East Pakistan, 1954
Letter 2

Do you remember the crumbling bricks of the house
where you were born—
>the balcony with rusted railing
>on the street with tea-shops like the one
>Nanabhai ran where
>at three you danced
>and begged for sips of sweet syrup?

You were always dancing
>to some tabla in your ears
>music unheard by others.

Decades later, I went back,
>surprised at the smallness of the place,
>the dark walls streaked with mold,
>the narrow, crowded streets.

Letter 3

I remember you on a stage
        in Armetola Maidan,
in a blue silk garara trimmed with gold,
        you hid behind the podium where Abbu stood.

He spoke into a megaphone
        to a crowd beyond your ability to count,
        my ability to imagine.

You were four,
        thrilled for the rare treat
        of going somewhere with Abbu.

You couldn't understand his words,
        I can't remember them—

only that dazzle of night and sound,
        distant glory,
the warmth of Abbu near,
        his voice a storm,
the field's echoing thunder.

Letter 4

You were four years, four months, and four days old,
new slate and chalk in hand,
dressed in blue silk,
your first lesson.

Dr. Shahidullah performed the ceremony:
recited Arabic, then Bengali,
prayed you would use language
for good, that words would guide your life.

He gently moved your finger holding chalk
across the slate—
> first, tracing "Bismillah" in Arabic,
> then your name in Bengali.

Perhaps your love of ritual started here.

Afterwards, there were laddus and smiles
from gathered family and friends.

And you never gave up the word.

Ammu, Saku, Amin Mama, Choiti, and Khalamma sitting on the verdanda in 72 Nazimudding Road.

Letter 5

72 Nazimuddin Road was the Lalbagh Fort,
    the Taj Mahal,
        whatever you wanted it to be.

Mango trees, banana stalks, and one guava trunk,
rose bushes in many colors,
purslane and mysterious greens in the kitchen garden,
pecked at by crows.

The veranda wrapped the front of the house —
each room connecting from it, or to it —
two bedrooms, a drawing room, and
on the other side of the yard — a stand-alone kitchen
with an earthen stove, holes for wood.

Iftar was on the stone floor of the veranda —
Nanni giving the first signal with *Bismillah,*
a glass of water, a date, and a prayer,
then Ammu, Khalamma, and Amin Mama.

You and Saku didn't fast in those days,
but broke fast alongside the grown-ups
    with solemn care.

Ammu, Choiti, Khalamma, Saku.

Letter 6

The veranda was the scene of many snaps.

Here you and Saku played tiddlywinks
      with cowrie shells,
patted your ceramic parrot,
plotted your next coup.

Ammu and Abbu stood there one night,
shouting, flinging pots.

Embedded in that instant the next fifty years—
      their rift,
         your future lives.

Another time you peered through window bars
      into the middle bedroom—
Amin Mama had locked the door.
You could hear Mamoni scream
      after each thud.

She had taken a rikshaw to New Market
with a fellow student, a boy—

another turning point
you didn't understand.
It took me decades.

Letter 7

After the theft,
policemen grabbed Shoaib, the servant boy,
beat him with their sticks.

He confessed to drugging us to sleep
so they could rob the house.

Shoaib wept, knees scraping stone slabs,
begged forgiveness for his crime,
melted veranda steps.

I wonder whether he was taken to the same prison
where Abbu spent years,
the one where Ammu took you to visit once,

where you waited in the front room.
A policeman gave you water in a dirty glass—
you paused, then drank to be polite.

To be precise, Shoaib wasn't really his name—
it was the name of another servant boy
from another time,
another place.

But this story could be true of all Shoaibs.

Letter 8

Ammu told bedtime stories every night,
    you and Saku tucked into her narrow bed.

Sometimes it was peris,
    heroic princes on flying peacock chariots,
rakhoshes, jinn,
    fierce retellings of ancient legends,

sometimes chapters in books we could not yet read,
or stories of her childhood and its hardships:
"The Bar of Soap" was one that mystified.

On the first of every month,
    when Nanabhai got paid,
    Boro Nani went shopping:

Mustard oil, sugar, and soap—
    one large bar for herself and her son,
    one small bar for Choto Nani and her four
        children—
    Ammu being the second child, the studious one.

This ritual shaped the contours of their lives:
    mustard oil for greens, but not fish,
        which had to be fried in its own belly fat,
    sugar locked up in Boro Nani's almirah,
        doled out *in extremis,*
    and soap for washing oneself, clothes, dishes—

but sparingly.

Ammu learned the morphology of power from soap:
By the end of the month—a world in time—
soap was a presence traced by absence.

Letter 9

Remember when you stole four annas to buy spicy chaat
        from the street vendor on Nazimuddin Road?
Forbidden—and so, irresistible.

Then you got sick—
        long pink worms wriggled inside your cheeks,
you swallowed the vile potion Doctor Shahib prescribed.

Once you lied
        about breaking the gramophone.

Saku owned up—she was cuddled and praised for
        honesty.
        You cringed, but still said nothing.

Then there was the time you took scissors
        to Ammu's Banarasi sari to make dresses for your
            dolls.
As punishment, she made you pull your own ears.

But still, you wrote a poem for her birthday,
        colored red flowers around the simple words,
        handed her the lined sheet with love.

Letter 10

Remember, too, the strange games the servants played with you and Saku?
> Shoaib before the theft.
> Even Nur Jehaner-Ma.

You didn't know then how to name it.
Never spoke of it to anyone but Saku.

Was it revenge of the servant class against the master's
> children?

Perhaps you didn't know trauma because you had no therapist
> to tell you
> how damaged you must be.

Perhaps the damage was so deep it became the real you.

Can this violence be rewritten to be expunged?

Karachi, West Pakistan, 1959
Letter 11

Camels were the first marvel,
    then elephants strolling the street.

You rode one.
    Each time he took a step
        a gigantic swaying motion rocked the
        tiny basket

where you perched with Saku and Ammu
    on an embroidered blanket,
        the handler holding what you thought was
        a stick.

The streets threw up dust and wonder.
    Ammu bought an ivory necklace
        and a brooch,

a carved wooden jewelry box
    inlaid with ivory,
        now hidden in my closet.

Can we be forgiven for these cruelties?
    Not knowing then what I know now?

I still cannot bear to burn the wretched jewels,
    the box—last gifts, years later, from Ammu.
I cannot erase the memory of that childhood ride—
    the joy of it.

Chicago, Illinois, 1959
Letter 12

O'Hare in a chilly September,
propellers slowing to a low whir,
tarmac rising beneath wide wings—
a new world thrust into your life.

Language failed you.
You clung to Ammu's sari.

On the first day of school Ammu walked between you and Saku
along the cold sidewalks.

On the second day, you held Saku's hand
and set off, fear snaking inside,
brave outside for Saku's sake.

The streets seemed long and dark,
the school far away.

You could read, but
the teacher's American accent baffled.

In kindergarten Saku broke down in tears
every morning for a week.
By 11 a.m., the teacher brought her to your class
where she sat sniffling till dismissal.

You patted her back,
held her hand.

A frugal intimacy.

Letter 13

Wrists crossed,
        fingers curled in a mudra,
your ankles tap to the tabla's beat,
        ghungroos jangling.

Somebody sings
        Hat tima tim tim
but you don't hear the words
        or see the dim rows,

you hear the rhythm of your feet
        stamping across the stage
the scent of marigolds scattering
        from your hair

as you twirl,
        the feel of hot lights on silk,
the oneness of sound,
        scent, and sway.

Choiti dancing in a Bengali-student-organized Celebration at the University of Chicago.

Ann Arbor, Michigan, 1960
Letter 14

You didn't know that you were an immigrant.

In summer, after breakfast, you did two hours of
        work:
    mostly math from next year's textbook,
    to get a head start, Mom said.

You are forgetting Bangla, Mom sighed,
    but didn't assign homework as remedy.
    She spoke in Bangla even when you replied in
        English.

Now I wonder how you could give up your mother
        tongue
  so easily.

Mom packed lunch in waxed paper: PB&J,
    or bologna and Miracle Whip on white bread,
    a Twinkie or Hostess cupcake,
    a small thermos of lemonade.

You threw the brown paper bag into the basket of your
        bike,
    rode up and down the neighborhood,
    collecting friends.

The five of you took off into the wilds of Ann Arbor
    exploring parks,
        abandoned fields by the railroad tracks,
        and once, all the way to the stone quarry
        where older kids met at night
        to drink beer.

You had to be home for supper by six.

Letter 15

How you loved those Twinkies in the lunchbox.

Today my three-card spread says there's a Twinkie in
my future again,
        since Mercury squares Saturn and conjoins the
                Sun,
or is it the Sun marking the Solstice?

In any case, it's a good day for spiritual activities
        and connecting deeply with cream-filled
                sponge-cake,
the kind from our high-school lunch bag,
        the kind which will outlast the apocalypse.

There's a corner of my taste buds
that still longs for the mushy sweetness you loved,

as if it could make me you again—
        lithe, lean, and full of promise—
as if I could reach out and touch the stars,
        as if the universe were not twirling away.

Letter 16

How strange the return to Nazimuddin Road—
language again a barrier—
as if the words which had been your friends for life
        were now strangers—
new lessons to recapture the lost language of birth.

Hard to use a latrine after flush toilets,
no hot running water.

You didn't get into Viqarunessa School for Girls,
because, the headmistress said,
you failed the English exam.

The exam tested mostly grammar, which you detested,
and the headmistress couldn't understand your midwestern twang.

You were home-schooled for the first time.
Nanni gave you strange advice.

Letter 17

Don't walk with your chest thrust out.
Lower your head, and
take small steps.

Don't talk too much;
girls should be modest
and quiet.

Above all,
don't go near a man—
or you'll end up with a baby.

When guests come for tea,
you keep to the far side of the room.

Lahore, West Pakistan, 1962
Letter 18

You and Saku arrived in Lahore
six months after Mom.

Much later, I understood why:
This gave skeptical in-laws time to know her,
unclouded by divorce,
>   two daughters living evidence of that shame.

You studied Urdu and Punjabi—
>   a different music to either Bengali or English.

Doing well in school didn't help.
Ajji's relatives were indifferent,
mildly contemptuous.

Baji-Gul said: *You may as well study,*
since you will never be pretty—
you are too short and too dark.

Letter 19

You and Saku took the bus to Queen Mary's College,
along with other girls from "Class B" families
who managed to get into the exclusive school.

You spoke English with native fluency—
though with an American accent—which the teachers
did their best to train out of your tongue.

The same bus where the girl who sat on the front seat
by the driver disappeared one day.
People whispered *s/he now went to the Boy's School.*

You stepped off the bus into a crowd of chauffeur-
           driven cars.
Accompanied by their Ayahs—these girls
dressed up their uniforms with white lace gloves.

You wore two sets of white uniforms by rotation—
two or three days running. The others wore
uniforms freshly starched and pressed every day.

At Tiffin time, you ate jam sandwiches Mom made;
the other girls bought hot meat pasties
and sweets from the Tiffin Wala.

In English class they struggled to make a sentence
with the word *book*, so you said:
I love to turn the musty pages of books in the library.

Letter 20

The summer was hot, 117 degrees by noon.
You stayed in the shade of the veranda.

Before leaving for work, Ajji assigned a topic:
> "If," "Abbottabad," "Jugnu" —
> each more enigmatic than the last.

You had to write an essay before you were free to
> read or play.

Saku wrote quick, pithy stories,
> then plunged into whatever book engrossed
> her.

You struggled, erased, crossed out, rewrote, and groaned.
> Stole looks at the unabridged
> *A Thousand and One Nights,*
> vaguely understood why it was forbidden.
> Vowed you'd never write again when grown
> up.

Later, these essays were published: *Of This and That,*
> your first book.

One day Apa-Gul made alu parathas and
pomegranate chutney,
> a treat for lunch.

You didn't know you'd never again eat all-natural
food
home-made from scratch,
not wrapped in cellophane.

Swat Valley, Northwest Frontier Province, 1963
Letter 21

Another hot summer. You and Saku roamed the steep
         slopes
looking for Saraswati while
Mother and Ajji taught English classes.

You ate breakfast in the Mess with the students.
The kind cook packed tiffin containers with pakoras
         and naan for lunch,
you thanked him with smiles, not speaking Pashto.

I don't remember what you did for hydration—
no bottles then—so perhaps you drank
the white water of the Swat River?

Each day you climbed a different hill,
imagined Sikander's army storming to Odigram and
         Barikot
decades before Ashoka conquered the Valley.

Two centuries later, Mahmoud of Ghazni
ended Hindu rule on Gandhara,
brought Islam to the Valley.

Proud you remembered something of lessons,
you saw everywhere the remnants of stupas,

temples, witness to a brutal history
even before the Taliban demolished the Buddhas,
threw acid on Malala's face—
acts of barbarism yet to come, prefigured.

But you were children
delighting in unaccustomed freedom,
relishing stony walks and cold streams—

history was something learned in textbooks
not something that would touch
your lives—not this summer, this perfect day.

Abbottabad, West Pakistan, 1964
Letter 22

One weekend Ajji drove the car
to Dil's Corner, Lower Malikpura, Abbottabad,
where Baji and Biji lived

just across the gulley from the
Waziristan Haveli, the high-walled compound
where almost six decades later

Osama Bin Laden would be gunned down.

That weekend you saw only the valley,
hills all around,
the scandal of wind and winter clouds.

You stood in the doorway of the small house,
wanted to roam the alleys,
but girls couldn't wander by themselves.

The canyon burned your eyes with longing.

Bloomington, Indiana, 1966
Letter 23

Never needing to stay up late
    because you didn't play—
        you were a natural at high school,
            reveled in inscrutable assignments,
                impossible deadlines . . .

You didn't always play fair.
    In English class,
        you argued with the teacher

and won, even when you hadn't
    read the poem being discussed,
        because you could.

You kept your side of the room neat—
    a struggle not to fight
        the clutter on the other side—
            Saku's wordless seething.

You were a nerd before you knew the word,
    the one who never climbed out the bedroom window at night,
        the one parents took for granted.

You were the blade never unsheathed.

Columbia, Missouri, 1967
Letter 24

The senior class Girls' Club invited you to join.
    What is the purpose of these meetings? you asked
        the dumbfounded faculty advisor.
      To have fun, she said.

Having decided to combine
    the last two years of high school into one,
      you said, *Thank you anyway,*
        I have classes at the university,

and I've joined Forensics Club.
    You loved Oratory, Poetry Interpretation,
      were assigned a debate partner
        who looked at you askance,

almost as if he knew
    that by the end of the year
      you would supplant him as valedictorian.

At the first away tournament your team won.
    In the hotel, you didn't realize
      only you and Saku had a room to
      yourselves—
        all other female debate team
        members
and the female faculty advisor shared the other room.

        After we returned the horrified headmaster
ruled
                all same-sex debate partners were to
                share a room
                      in future tournaments,

and no more than four to a room.
        More space and quiet, you thought, to prepare.
            Decades later, I understood.

Perhaps it was the strangeness of our shalwar-kameez.
Perhaps the English accent.
Perhaps the color of our skin.

Shaheen as a freshman at Vassar.

Poughkeepsie, New York, 1968
Letter 25

Getting off the plane alone at JFK,
    a terrifying first,
taking the Vassar bus from the airport,
    another.

Do you remember the thrill and fear
    of being free—
nausea knotting with exhilaration
    in your gut?

Those evenings in the hallway of the fifth floor,
    learning to swear like deckhands—
Karen, Leslie, Judi, Joan,
    Cecily, Marilyn, and Susan.

You couldn't believe the luck—
    in a place Mom thought was safe
because it was only for girls,
    but what girls!

They opened your eyes
    to boys, wine, movies,
first a room of one's own,
    then a mind.

Letter 26

During Orientation we were assigned
    a group faculty advisor,
who took us outside
    under a spreading oak for counseling.

He said
    it didn't much matter
what we studied:
    since we would all marry and have children.

So you picked fun,
made up your own eclectic major.

Signs, symbols, and symbolic detail—
    the English Department opened the world:
Flaubert, Emily Dickinson, Turgenev,
    Edna St. Vincent Millay.

Later you added Chinua Achebe,
    Mirabai,
Anna Akhmatova, Yeats, Dylan Thomas,
    the Bhagavad Gita.

Letter 27

Second semester transfer boys appeared,
    sharing floors
though not bathrooms—
    that came later.

Mom wrote furious letters
    to the President,
the Dean of Students,
    even the Board of Trustees.

To no avail—
    Vassar went co-ed
and you stayed—
    the scholarship an unbreakable tie.

The fifth floor group: Joan, Marilyn, Judi, Karen, Leslie, Susan.

Letter 28

You were an exotic distraction.
        Busloads of boys
Yale and Princeton
        delivered for the weekend dance.

Once your roommate had a party in your suite
        Susan encouraged you to skip.
Given your workload it seemed sensible—
        years later I understood.

You were a brown girl in a white world,
        but you didn't know it.

Boston, Massachusetts, 1969
Letter 29

Karen and you went to Cambridge for a weekend
>to visit her boyfriend.

You didn't have one,
>just hung out with the others.

Before leaving
>his gay roommate said,

Meeting you makes me wish
>*that I was straight.*

You wondered
>whether Baji-Gul might have been wrong.

We hitchhiked back to Poughkeepsie.

New York, New York, 1969
Letter 30

Leslie, Joan and you took the Vassar bus to New York,
    stayed at the approved hotel.

You wore the sari Mom gave you for going to college—
    a daring first.

It fell apart on the elevator going up the Empire State Building.

Luckily there were still phone booths then.

At the top,
you bolted into a booth like Superman,
while the others stood guard outside.

Several safety pins did the job.

The next time you went to New York
you borrowed a dress from Leslie.

Poughkeepsie, New York, 1969
Letter 31

Our poems burned on the bridge
    over Sunset Lake—
edges curling to the sky
    like a prayer gone wrong.

The match flickered, your fingers
    scorched like songs
not ready for the madness of light,
    the nearness of others

who could not know this secret life,
    this scent of smoke—
this trembling on the brink
    of a run not started,

this brief encounter
    with divinity.

Letter 32

You met Nicolaas—
      a trivial circumstance.

You smoked Schimmelpennincks
      in smoke-filled rooms

by way of self defense
      but also liked the shock effect,

if you were honest—
      you didn't inhale.

You watched ashes wink.

Washington, D.C, 1971
Letter 33

Your first place was a room in a boarding house.
This didn't last long;
a man tried to force the door your first week.

Luckily the Super heard your screams—
came running to chase the guy out.

You found a basement apartment near Dupont Circle.
Your roommate dragged in an abandoned dinette set
            from the street,
sewed colorful covers for the matching chairs.

You learned to make tuna-fish spaghetti,
ate two hotdogs with chips every day for lunch.

You had books on the built-in bookcase,
a mattress on the floor.

Letter 34

Nobody mocked your shalwar-kameez.
Guys asked you out.
There was easy camaraderie
among the students.

You debated nationalism:
was there need for a common language,
common religion,
common ethnicity?
Or was identity defined when
legal and emotional boundaries were co-terminus?

While you discussed,
      Pakistan fell apart.

Your dream of joining the Foreign Service
(then closed to women—but of course you would
              storm it)
became remote.

You read the inaugural issue of *Ms. Magazine*,
The Feminine Mystique.

You ate calamari for the first time,
went on long walks in Kalorama Circle,
learned to say *Ciao* and *Arrivederci*.

Letter 35

A fellow student said, *It's hard to explain you to my wife—
 brilliant, beautiful, and nice.*

You decided then
that Baji-Gul had been wrong.

You bought American slacks and tops,
discarded shalwar-kameez,
but only at school.

Letter 36

Remember dinners at the Browns—
those sparkling nights!
The guests an eclectic bunch—some academics,
some diplomats—witty and urbane—
That Inn at Avignon! The bridge at Giverny!

Nicolaas complained that you smiled at Professor
               Brown.
How could you not?
The senior Brown was gallant and gray,
told enchanting stories and danced.

Nico should have worried instead about Max,
who stared at you through every seminar.

How did you know
that if you crooked a finger,
Max would lope to your side
with long strides?

You and Nicolaas broke up on Friday
before the annual SAIS dance.

You went to the dance anyway.

That night, your housemates climbed the transom to see
whether Max stayed over.

Letter 37

On Saturday evenings you went to Mass with Serenella
so she could sleep in on Sundays.

St. Matthew's Cathedral radiant with ceremony:
incense, costumed processions, Latin mass,
      and glorious, mysterious music.

How you longed to belong to that pageantry!

If only Islam had glamor.

Letter 38

Nicolaas's postdoc at the Smithsonian ended.
He got another postdoc at Oxford,
said it would be good for your relationship
to be separated for a year.

You saw him off at Dulles Airport.

You spent three nights and three days on the floor of
                your apartment —
the ceremonies of grief a crucible
you barely understood.

Princeton, New Jersey, 1973
Letter 39

There must have been a Cazimi in the cosmos that
September
when you entered the grounds not as a guest but a
resident.

The old GC black and tower like, mimicking castles,
Procter Hall with gargoyles on the wall,
one grotesque mouth holding a bar of soap.

Organ music signaled the procession to dinner at 6:30
p.m.,
black academic gowns billowing over jeans and tees,
slouching at long tables.

Almost at once you argued with a guy across the
table,
so supremely annoying the discussion never ended—
even half a century later.

Letter 40

Late at night,
after a freezing rain,
we walked to the midnight show:
the path was treacherous,
the world a miracle of white—
white diamonds hung
on white branches of trees
reaching to the white ground,
everywhere a blinding white—
the late moon's light
magnified by a prism of ice
on ice on ice.

Letter 41

Long days in the Firestone stacks
punctuated by study breaks and jelly doughnuts.

Evenings in the Debasement Bar
debating everything from punk rock to politics.

Eventually you wrote a "Dear John" letter,
explaining the argumentative friend might just be
more.

Suddenly Nico found time to fly to Princeton,
begged you to change your mind,
said he added your name to his bank account.

He offered you a sedative.
You declined.

Shaheen and Mom

Letter 42

You sent a letter to Mom and Ajji,
who were then in Pakistan,
asking if they would agree to meet Clark.

He is a scholar of 18th century German literature, you wrote,
Ph.D. from Princeton and Assistant Professor at Harvard,
a gentle man, and Jewish.

The only word they heard was *Jewish.*

I still marvel at your naivete—
would it have turned out otherwise
I wonder
      if the letter had been sent
           later
                to San Diego
                      away from prying Pakistani
            eyes?

Brute honesty was your first impulse.
Perhaps that was foolishness.

Letter 43

Ajji, who told you on long walks
we were all citizens of the world;
we were born Muslim
but all monotheistic religions were true believers—

that same Ajji, who taught you cosmopolitanism
was the highest world order,
who reminded you
that Pakistan was the first country to recognize Israel—

that self-same Ajji disowned you,
forbade Mom from speaking with you,
or attending your wedding.

For once, Mom defied Ajji.
She came,
cried most of the three days, as did you—
prolepsis of asthma and the hard years to come:
I still struggle with breath;
insomnia
became my intermittent friend.

Nevertheless, you were married in the Rose Garden
in Princeton in June, on a brilliant day—
the scent of roses everywhere, the sun relentless.

Clark and Shaheen's wedding picture.

Notes and Asides

Choiti is my childhood nickname—an affectionate diminutive for the Bengali month of Choitra, when I was born.

Armetola Maidan is the name of a huge field in Dhaka where many political events were held during the elections of 1954. It has a capacity of over 50,000.

A garara is an outfit often worn in South India, also used for children in Dhaka in those days.

My father was Shamsul Haque, the first secretary-general of the Awami League, member of parliament from Tangail, and pivotal in instigating the Bengali National Language Movement. He was imprisoned by the Pakistani Government multiple times for these activities.

Our family combined elements of the Muslim "Bismillah" ceremony with the Bengali "Hathe Khori" ceremony to begin my education—first in Arabic, then in Bengali. I was lucky to have mine performed by Dr. Shahidullah, one of the most eminent Bengali scholars of the day. I didn't study English, however, until a year later when I started kindergarten at a Catholic Girls' School.

Some Bengali words:
 Abbu: an affectionate diminutive for abba, or father
 Ammu: an affectionate diminutive for amma, or mother
 Laddu: a yellow ball-shaped dessert served on celebratory occasions
 Nanni: grandmother
 Khalamma: maternal aunt
 Mama: maternal uncle
 Mamoni: wife of maternal uncle
 Iftar: breaking fast in the evening during Ramadan
 peri: a Bengali fairy
 rakhosh: a man-eating ogre
 jinn: a muslim genie (although they can be either believers or non-believers)
 Nanabhai: maternal grandfather
 Boro Nani: "big grandmother," the senior wife in a dual wife household
 Choto Nani: "little grandmother," the junior wife in a dual wife household
 Ayah: nurse or babysitter, usually live-in
 tabla: South Asian drums
 ghungroos: heavy silver anklets which jingle when you dance or walk

Shahib was a word used under the British Raj for Englishmen. Later, it became a form of honorific address for any male figure of authority or high station. So we addressed the medical doctor not by his surname, but simply as Doctor Shahib.

A mudra is the ritual positioning of the hands and fingers (sometimes the entire body) in South Asian dance. It also has spiritual meaning in Hinduism and Buddhism.

Saku: my younger sister's nickname, an abbreviation of Saeqa, which means bolt of lightning.

Shoaib: a male name of Arabic origin that means *one who shows the right path*. It is the alternate Arabic transcription of Shuaib, derived from the name of a Midianite prophet mentioned in the Qur'an who is often associated with the biblical figure Jethro. It is also the name of a male servant boy.

Nur-Jehaner-Ma: translates as mother of the light of the world. It was the name of a woman who was a cook in our house for thirty years.

Some Urdu/Punjabi words:
    Ajji: an abbreviation of abbaji, or honored father. This is how my sister and I addressed our stepfather
    Baji: another abbreviation of abbaji, which everyone called Ajji's father
    Biji: an abbreviation of ammaji, which everyone called Ajji's mother
    Baji-Gul: Flower Sister. Ajji's nickname for his second sister

Apa-Gul: Flower Sister. Nickname for his eldest sister

Shalwar-kameez: the loose pantaloons and tunic with a dupatta, or long scarf, worn by girls and women in South Asia

Hat tima tim tim is the first line of a Bengali nursery rhyme which was put to music for dancing.

Divorce is allowed in Islam, but in those days, there was a great deal of stigma attached to it in South Asia. Decades later, living in the United States, Apa-Gul still referred to my mother disparagingly as "a divorced woman."

Saraswati is the Hindu goddess of education and learning.

Sikander is the Bengali name for Alexander the Great. It was my maternal grandfather's name and later became my son's middle name.

Waziristan Haveli is the name of the walled mansion in Abbottabad where Osama Bin Laden hid for five years. My stepfather's family home was across the gulley from this mansion.

St. Matthew's Cathedral is the seat of the Archbishop of the Roman Catholic Archdiocese of Washington D.C. A historic landmark, it is known for having one of the most beautiful church interiors of modern times. In those days, Mass was always in Latin.

Cazimi is an astrological term that refers to a planet transiting between 0-1 degrees from the sun, or "the heart of the sun." This conjunction between the transiting planet and the luminary enhances the power of whichever planet is involved.

GC is the nickname for the Graduate College Dormitory in Princeton.

Procter Hall was the main dining room in the GC. And yes, in those ancient days we really did process into dinner in black academic gowns to the sound of organ music.

About the Author

Shaheen Dil is a reformed academic, banker and consultant who now devotes herself to poetry. She was born in Bangladesh and lives in Pittsburgh. Her poems have been widely published in literary journals and anthologies. Her poem "River at Night" was a winning poem in the *Passager* 2021 Poetry Contest. Her work was nominated for a Pushcart prize. Dil has published two books of poetry, *Acts of Deference* (Fakel 2016) and *The Boatmaker's Art* (Kelsay Books 2024.) Dil is a member of the Pittsburgh Poetry Exchange, the DVP/US1 Poets, and the Porch Poets. She holds a BA from Vassar College, a master's degree from Johns Hopkins University, and a Ph.D. from Princeton University. Additional information is available on her website: shaheendil.com.

Author photo by JMKL Creative

Gyroscope Press
Constance Brewer, Publisher
PO Box 1989
Gillette, WY 82718
gyroscopepress@gmail.com

Made in the USA
Columbia, SC
21 April 2025